Anonymous

Oration of Hon. O. P. Morton,

address of Major-General George G. Meade, and poem of Bayard Taylor,

together with the other exercises at the dedication of the monuments in

the soldiers' national cemetery at Gettysburg, July 1st, 1869

Anonymous

Oration of Hon. O. P. Morton,
address of Major-General George G. Meade, and poem of Bayard Taylor, together with the other exercises at the dedication of the monuments in the soldiers' national cemetery at Gettysburg, July 1st, 1869

ISBN/EAN: 9783337308049

Printed in Europe, USA, Canada, Australia, Japan

Cover: Foto ©ninafisch / pixelio.de

More available books at **www.hansebooks.com**

ORATION

OF

HON. O. P. MORTON,

ADDRESS

OF

MAJOR GENERAL GEORGE G. MEADE,

AND

POEM

OF

BAYARD TAYLOR,

TOGETHER WITH THE OTHER EXERCISES AT THE DEDICA-
TION OF THE MONUMENT IN THE SOLDIERS' NATIONAL
CEMETERY AT GETTYSBURG, JULY 1ST, 1869.

PUBLISHED BY THE ASSOCIATION.

GETTYSBURG:

J. E. WIBLE, PRINTER, NORTH-EAST COR. OF WASHINGTON & R. R. STS,
1870.

PRAYER

REV. HENRY WARD BEECHER.

Lord God of our fathers, we thank Thee that
Thou hast been God of this land; that Thou
hast inspired our citizens to frame wise laws
and lay the foundation of intelligence and of virtue
and of piety. We thank Thee that Thou hast ordained among us institutions for the benefit of all,
and in all the history of their formation, and amidst
all the struggles through which they have passed,
Thou hast been on the side of liberty and knowledge, and hast befriended the poor and needy.
We thank Thee, O Lord our God, that when times
of struggle came on; when evil rushed in upon us
like a flood, Thou didst at last raise up opposition,
and didst call from all places those that should assert again the everlasting truths of human right and
human liberty. And when aggression broke forth
into battle, Thou, O Lord God of our fathers, didst

call forth from all our fields, from towns, and from cities, multitudes innumerable, who stood heroically to defend this nation and maintain its integrity unimpaired, and here, within this eminence, where Thou didst lead Thy people unto victory, we are gathered again to renew associations and derive instruction, and hand down to our posterity lessons of patriotism and heroic devotion which here were given. Grant, we beseech of Thee, Thy blessing to rest upon all who are gathered here to-day. O Lord, we cannot ask Thy blessing upon those that rest in sleep in death round about us, whom Thou hast blessed, for we humbly trust in Jesus Christ—in the immortality of another and better land. But, O Lord, remember that all our hearts yet bleed for them. Remember those whose home is poorer since they died. May they be cheered in recollecting that their whole land is richer. O Lord, bless those fathers whose sons lie buried here, and mothers into whose hearts the sword entered more deeply than into theirs who were slain thereby. Remember the orphan children of those that are silent here; and we beseech of Thee that wherever they are, and under whatsoever circumstances surrounded, they may feel not only the sympathy and good-will of their fellow-citizens, but, in an eminent degree, may Thy providence smile upon them. May the soldiers' children never prove unworthy of their fathers' name; may they grow up into true heroism and love of their native land, and, as did their fathers, let them be willing to shed their blood, to lay down their lives, for the sake of their country. Let Thy blessing, O Lord, rest upon Thy servant who commanded here in time of great trial, and whose life mercifully has been spared through intervening years since, to be here again under circumstances so different. Long may his life be spared, and those of his household, and may Thy blessing make him instrumental for right; and for the good of the whole land, may it come back in measure upon him and his! Remember all who were here associated with him in command, not only so many as are now present, but those who are detained from this ground. Wherever any are, may the blessings of Almighty God rest upon them and theirs, and their families. Remember, O Lord, the soldiers who fought here and everywhere; we pray for them and theirs, that God's blessing may attend them to the end of life; save them from snares and temptations mightier than their virtue, and grant that in all their manifest and noble endeavors, they may achieve yet more than is contained on the record of their past. We beseech Thee, Lord God, to grant Thy blessing upon this whole nation; be pleased to unite together the hearts of this once divided but now united people;

unite their hearts together, and with these new foundations of liberty, universal intelligence, and virtue and piety, may this Union grow stronger than it was or could have been. And though we have been shaken with a mighty shaking; though with the ploughshare of war Thou hast passed through our fields, grant that hereafter the harvest may be more abundant than it could have been without this Thy culture. We beseech Thee, O God, to pour Thy blessing upon the President of the United States, and all that are associated with him in council and administration. May their lives and health be precious in Thy sight; may discretion be given them from on high; may a prosperous issue be given to all work of their hands undertaken in behalf of this land. Bless, O Lord, the army and navy of the United States; in all their labors and efforts may they still uphold the banner of the country; not in a spirit of pride or of wanton aggression, but may they see in our flag justice, order, and liberty for all, prosperity with virtue, until around and around the world, as every wind shall bear its folds, men may be told what liberty and true piety does for a nation. Strengthen the weak with strength against the strong. Counsel with Thy counsel against the oppressor, although the earth overturn and overturn until the right is established. Grant Thy blessing to rest upon all that are here, and upon the great body of citizens throughout all the United States, and upon the whole family of man. Grant that need of war shall cease and Gentile and Jew be gathered together in harmony, and the whole earth see Thy salvation. All of which we humbly ask in the adorable name of the Lord Jesus, our Saviour, to whom, with the Father and the Holy Spirit, we will give praise forever. Amen.

ADDRESS

BY

MAJ. GEN. GEORGE G. MEADE.

My Fellow Citizens, Ladies and Gentlemen:

Six years ago I stood upon this ground under circumstances very different from those which now surround us. These beautiful hills and valleys, teeming with luxuriant crops, these happy faces around me, are widely different from the tumultuous roar of war and the terrible scenes enacted at that time. Four years ago I stood here, by invitation of some honorable gentlemen who have brought me here this time, and laid the corner-stone of the Monument which we are brought here to-day to dedicate; and now, for the third time, I appear before you at the request of the managers of the Monument Association to render my assistance, humble as it is, in paying respect to the memory of the brave men who fell here, by dedicating this Monument to them; and at the request of these gentlemen I am about to make to you a few, a very few, remarks which are incident to this occasion and suggested by it. When I look around and see, as I now see, so-many brave men who were by my side in that memorable battle, among them his Excellency the present Governor of Pennsylvania, General Geary, and others who were with me at that time; when I look back and think upon the noble spirits who then fought so well, and now sleep that sleep that knows no waking—gallant Reynolds, my bosom friend, as well as my right-hand officer; brave Vincent, and Zook, and Weed, and others, far more in number than I have time or words to mention—my feelings are those of mingled sadness and joy—sadness, my friends, to think that there ever was an occasion when such men should be arrayed in battle, as they were here; that we should ever have been called upon, as we were upon this field, to defend the flag of our country and Government, which had been handed down to us from our forefathers. It is sad to think of the mourning and desolation which prostrated our whole land, North and South; it is sad to contemplate the vast destruction of life which we here wrought in obedience to our highest duty. I am filled with sadness to think of the host of mourning widows and orphans left throughout the land by that dreadful struggle. Such thoughts necessarily crowd upon us. At the same time I give thanks to the Almighty, who directed the event, and who selected me as an humble

2

instrument, with those then around me upon this
field, to obtain that decisive victory which turned
the tide of that great war, and settled forever the
trust in this country of the great principles of per-
sonal liberty and constitutional freedom. I feel
grateful, too, that our fellow countrymen have been
moved to such respect and honor as we are now
paying to the memory of those men who, in the dis-
charge of their duty, laid down their lives, proving,
by the highest sacrifice man can render, their devotion to the cause they were defending. Gratitude
to those present to-day, who, by their presence, con-
tribute to render the high honor justly due to the
fallen brave. There is one subject, my friends,
which I will mention now and on this spot, while my
attention is being called to it, and on which I trust
my feeble voice will have some influence. When
I contemplate this field, I see here and there the
marks of hastily dug trenches in which repose the
dead against whom we fought. They are the work
of my brothers in arms the day after the battle.
Above them a bit of plank indicates simply that
these remains of the fallen were hurriedly laid there
by soldiers who met them in battle. Why should
we not collect them in some suitable place? I do
not ask that a monument be erected over them; I
do not ask that we should in any way endorse their
cause or their conduct, or entertain other than feel-

ings of condemnation for their course; but they are dead! They have gone before their Maker to be judged. In all civilized countries it is the usage to bury the dead with decency and respect, and even to fallen enemies respectful burial is accorded in death. I earnestly hope that this suggestion may have some influence throughout our broad land, for this is only one of a hundred crowded battle-fields. Some persons may be designated by the Government to collect these neglected bones and bury them without commemorating monuments, simply indicating that below sleep misguided men who fell in battle for a cause over which we triumphed. I shall delay you no longer, for you are about to listen to one of the most eloquent men in this country. My purpose was simply to comply with the kind invitation given me to speak meet words of praise for the dead heroes sleeping around, and to aid in the solemnities of this occasion. I thank you for your attention, and will now unveil the statue.

ORATION

OF

GOVERNOR O. P. MORTON.

When the Monument we are about to dedicate shall have crumbled into dust; when the last vestige of this Cemetery shall have been obliterated by the the hand of time; when there shall be nothing left of all that we see now but the hills, the valleys, the streams, and the distant mountains, the great battle which here took place, with its far-reaching consequences, will still live in history. Nations have their birth, youth, maturity, old age and death; and ours, though we call it eternal, and our institutions immortal, will be no exception. But though nations must pass away, and all physical evidence of their existence be lost, yet may they live through all time in the brightness of their examples, in the glory of their deeds, and in the beneficence of their institutions. These are the inheritances they leave to the far-coming centuries.

When the pyramids of Egypt shall have sunk to the level of the Nile; when the last remnant of

Grecian architecture, the last inscribed block of marble, shall have perished, men will still read of Moses and the Pass of Thermopylæ. Monuments, after all, are but for the present, and may only instruct a few generations. But a glorious deed is a joy forever.

Six years ago, day after to-morrow, the Union army was stretched along these heights from Culp's Hill to Round Top—a human breakwater, against which the great tidal wave of rebellion was to dash in vain, and be thrown back in bloody spray and broken billows. The rebel chieftain, flushed by his success at Fredericksburg and Chancellorsville, forgetting that his triumphs had arisen from the fact that he had fought upon his own soil, behind natural fastnesses, having the advantage of choice of position and knowledge of the country, had insolently crossed the Potomac and invaded the loyal State of Pennsylvania. But from this invasion he was hurled back in bloody defeat, and in disordered flight crossed the Potomac, never again to set foot upon the soil of a loyal State. On yonder high ground across the plain was drawn out in battle array the rebel host. It was an open field; the terms were nearly equal; and steady Northern valor, animated by the love of country, was to meet the boasted chivalry of the South fighting for slavery, sweep it from the field, strip it of its mere tricious plumes, and give the Confederacy a fatal wound.

It is the solid qualities of men and nations that win in the long run. The chivalry of false pride, the arrogance and vanity of a favored class, whose elevation is only seen by the depression of others, may, by spasmodic efforts for a time dazzle the eyes of the world, but cannot long maintain a successful contest with truth, justice, and the strength of free institutions. This was illustrated in the war of the rebellion, and in the battle of Gettysburg. This battle was not won by superior strategy or military genius, although managed with great courage and skill by General Meade and his subordinate commanders, who left nothing undone that the occasion seemed to require, and who made the best use of the forces and opportunities at their command.

It was a three days' battle, with varying fortunes the first and second days, in which the steadiness of Northern valor, animated by the convictions of a just cause, and the love and pride of a great and free country, finally wore out, bore down, and swept from the field the rebel masses, composed of men of equal physical courage, but whose moral powers were impaired by the absence of that strong conviction of the right which is a vast element of success.

In yonder Cemetery, among the white tombstones, "where heaves the turf in many a mouldering heap"

over the buried generations of the hamlet, was
planted the artillery whose fearful peals would have
aroused the slumbering dead were it not ordained
that they should awake only at the sound of the
last trump. Just behind the crest of the hill, in the
old cemetery, stood the tent of our glorious com-
mander, the imperturbable Meade, calmly dictating
his orders, while the storm of shot and shell flew
over and around him. From yonder steeple, south-
west of the village, the rebel chieftain surveyed the
field, directed his host, and from time to time saw
his advancing columns reel and wither, and finally
retreat in hopeless flight and confusion. The
flower of the rebel army had been chosen for the
assault, and were massed to bring overwhelming
numbers to bear on the point of attack. The rebel
chieftain brought together more than one hundred
and fifty pieces of artillery, with which, for three
hours, he poured a terrific fire upon that part of the
Union lines he intended to assault.

It was a grand and solemn sight, when line after
line, with steady step and in perfect order, emerged
from the smoke and swept across the field toward
the Union army. It was a moment of vast peril
and import, of which both parties were powerfully
conscious. If the rebel assault was successful, and
we lost the battle, Washington and Philadelphia
were within their grasp. The North invaded, de-

feated, and demoralized would do—we know not what. Foreign nations would be encouraged to intervene, and the South, elated, 'would put forth more desperate efforts than before. If the assault failed, and we gained the battle, the remnant of the rebel hosts must seek safety in flight, and a blow would be inflicted upon the Confederacy from which it could scarcely recover. These thoughts were present in the minds of all, and gave heroic courage to assault and to resist. But now the fire of our artillery was opened upon the advancing columns, and the shot and shell tore through their ranks, making great gaps, which were quickly filled up by those who came behind. But onward they came with desperate courage, until soon the fierce fire of musketry on both sides mingled with the horrid roar of artillery. Then, with terrific yells, they rushed upon our lines; but the impetus of their assault was suddenly checked. They were met with a courage as desperate as their own, and a fierce hand-to-hand conflict took place. The result was not long doubtful. Their thinned and broken columns were flung back across the plain in headlong flight, leaving thousands of prisoners in our hands, the ground covered with dead and dying, and wet and muddy with blood. We had gained the day, though at fearful cost. The victory was great and mighty in its consequences. The prestige of the rebel army was broken, never to be recovered, and the wound inflicted upon the Confederacy was never staunched until it had bled to death.

The next day was the 4th of July, and the most memorable since that of 1776. On another field it witnessed the surrender of another large rebel army to the great chieftain of the war, now our illustrious President. The capture of Vicksburg opened the navigation of the Mississippi river, and severed from the Confederacy all that part of its territory lying west of that river. The loss to the Confederacy was irreparable. It was cut off from its chief source of supplies. The limits of the war were greatly circumscribed. The mass of the rebel population was demoralized, and began to despair. From that day it became manifest that the rebellion could not succeed, unless the Southern people exhibited that endurance, patience under adversity, and high devotion that will sacrifice everything for the cause, which, as it turned out, they did not possess. By our victories at Gettysburg and Vicksburg the rebellion lost its prestige in Europe, and all hopes of foreign intervention.

At the foot of the Monument sleep the heroes of the battle. Here lies the father, the husband, the brother and the only son. In far off homes, among the hills of New England, on the shores of the lakes and in the valleys and plains of the West, the widow, the orphan, and the aged parents are weeping for these beloved dead. Many of the tombs are marked "unknown," but they will all be recognized on the morning of the Resurrection. The unknown dead left behind them kindred, friends, and breaking hearts. None die so humble but leave some one to mourn. "Perished at Gettysburg, in defense of their country," nine hundred and seventy-nine men of whose names, homes, or lineage there is no trace left on earth. Doubtless the Recording Angel has preserved the record, and when the books are opened on the last day their names will be found in letters of light on the immortal page of heroes who died that their country might live.

In the fields before us are the graves of the rebel dead, now sunk to the level of the plain, "unmarked, unhonored, and unknown." They were our countrymen—of our blood, language, and history. They displayed a courage worthy of their country, and of a better cause, and we may drop a tear to their memory. The news of this fatal field carried agony to thousands of Southern homes, and the wail of despair was heard in the everglades and orange groves of the South. Would to God that these men had died for their country and not in fratricidal strife, for its destruction. Oh, who can describe the wickedness of rebellion, or paint the horrors of civil war!

The rebellion was madness. It was the insanity of States, the delirium of millions, brought on by the pernicious influence of human slavery. The people of the South were drunk with the spoils of the labor of four millions of slaves. They were educated in the belief that chivalry and glory were the inheritance only of slaveholders; that free institutions and free labor begat cowardice and servility; that Northern men were sordid and mercenary, intent only upon gain, and would not fight for their Government or principles. And thus educated, and thus believing, they raised their hands to strike the Government of their fathers and to establish a new constitution, the chief corner-stone of which was to be human slavery.

The lust of power, the unholy greed of slavery, the mad ambition of disappointed statesmen impelled the people of the South to a fearful crime, which drenched the land with fraternal blood, that has been punished as few crimes have ever been in this world, but out of which, we are assured, that God, in his providence will bring forth the choicest blessings to our country and to the human race; even as of the dead. Liberty universal, soon to be guaranteed and preserved by suffrage universal; the keeping of a nation's freedom to be entrusted to *all the people*, and not to a part only; the national reproach washed out in rivers of blood, it is true; but

the sins of the world were atoned by the blood of
the Saviour, and the expiation of blood seems to be
the grand economy of God founded in wisdom, to
mortals inscrutable. Resurrection comes only from
the grave. Death is the great progenitor of life.
From the tomb of the rebellion a nation has been
born again. The principles of liberty, so gloriously
stated in the Declaration of Independence, had
hitherto existed in theory. The Government had
ever been a painful contradiction to the Declaration.
While proclaiming to the world that liberty was the
gift of God to every human being, four millions of
the people were held in abject and brutalizing slavery, under the shadow of the national flag. In the
presence of these slaves, professions of devotion to
liberty were vain and hypocritical. The clanking of
their chains ascended perpetually in contradiction to
our professions, and the enemies of republicanism
pointed contemptuously to our example. But all
this is passed. Slavery lies buried in the tomb of
the rebellion. The rebellion, the offspring of slavery,
hath murdered its unnatural parent, and the perfect
reign of liberty is at hand.

With the ratification of the fifteenth article, pro-
posed by Congress as an amendment to the Constitution of the United States, which we have every
reason to believe will soon be completed, impartial
suffrage will be established throughout the land.

The equal rights of men will be recognized, and the millennium in liberty and government will be realized, to which our fathers looked forward with hopefulness and joy.

The principles of liberty once planted in the earth, and ripened into their rich fruits, will be borne through all the ages, blessing mankind to the latest generation, even as the seeds first sown by the hand of God in Paradise, were blown by the winds from continent to continent, until the world was clothed with verdure, fruits, and flowers.

The prospect for liberty throughout the world was never so bright as it is to-day. In all civilized lands the grand armies of freedom are on their march. And they are allied armies. Victory to one will give prestige and confidence to the others. With some, progress will be slow; they will encounter disaster and defeat, but will again rally, and go forward to final victory. In the great campaign of freedom we count, not by months, but by decades and generations, in which there will be many a Bull Run, many a Gettysburg, and a final Appomattox. The lines of march will be marked by many a cemetery like this, by the wrecks of fallen institutions and dynasties, and by the ruins of hereditary privilege and caste.

Let us briefly review the advance of liberty since 1776.

The principles of the Declaration of Independence took early and deep root in France. The people of the empire had long suffered from the grossest misrule and oppression, and their minds were well prepared to comprehend and accept the new Gospel of Liberty. The French revolution first threw off the kingly government, then established complete democracy, but not knowing how to use liberty without abusing it, the people being governed by their passions, and seeking to avenge upon parties and classes the wrongs they had suffered for generations, passed into anarchy, from which the transition back to monarchy and despotism was easy and rapid. But the return of monarchy was not characterized by the former oppression and misrule. The people had learned their rights and monarchs had learned their power. Many of the old abuses which had been swept away by the revolution were gone forever, and the new monarchy governed with comparative justice, liberality, and humanity.

The spirit of liberty had entered into the hearts of the people, and from time to time asserted itself in various ways, and in 1848 France returned again to a republic. This lasted but a short time, but the new monarch who overthrew it and established himself upon its ruins was constrained to acknowledge the sovereignty of the people, and to profess to accept his crown by the vote of the majority. While we cannot say much for the freedom of that election, nor believe that the result was the will of the people, yet it was of vast significance that the usurping government was compelled to claim its title from a pretended popular election. In many respects the government of Napoleon III has been excellent. He has recognized the freedom of religious opinion. He has protected the people in their persons and property. He has encouraged trade and industry, stimulated manufactures, and extended their commerce. He has given them a constitution which creates a legislative body, and guarantees many rights and privileges. But the people are not satisfied. They are denied liberty of speech and of the press on political questions. They are not allowed to assemble for the discussion of measures in which they are vitally interested. Their legislative body is so constructed and managed as to be a mere registry of the will of the Emperor. The recent elections show the spirit of discontent and the existence of a powerful party who understand their rights and are determined to assert them, peaceably, if they can, and, as we have reason to believe, forcibly, if they must. The attentive observer, and student of French history, is led to the conclusion that nothing can preserve the throne and dynasty of Napoleon III, but the concession of the popular rights and the establishment of freedom of speech and of the press, of the elections, and of the legislative body.

The republican sentiment of France, though it has been unfortunate, and from time to time suppressed and apparently extinguished, is still vital, is growing in intelligence and power, and cannot be restrained, unless monarchy becomes so liberal and free as to confer the substantial benefit of a republic.

We cannot doubt that Napoleòn appreciates the situation, and is preparing to make such concessions as will keep the popular discontent this side of revolution.

The march of liberty in Germany is slow but steady. The great German family are struggling for unity and freedom. The institutions of Germany are becoming more liberal from year to year, and the condition of the people better and happier.

The evil of large standing armies, annually withdrawing the young men from home and productive pursuits, is still endured, because Germany is surrounded by warlike and powerful enemies, clad in complete armor.

But everywhere the tendency of the German mind is to the fullest liberty of thought, and to the recognition of the "equal rights" of men.

Austria, so long oppressed, reels and responds to the impulse of liberty. An intelligent Emperor, who has not shut his eyes to what is going on in the world around him, perceives that he cannot stem the powerful current everywhere setting in toward free institutions, and that the security of his throne depends upon his conceding to the people rights and privileges which have been denied them since Austria was an empire, and giving back to Hungary the enjoyment of her ancient constitution. The abolition of the Concordat, the establishment of religious freedom, the equal taxation of all classes, are among the hopeful beginnings of Austrian reform.

Italy, the ancient seat of the power and glory of the Roman Empire, land of history, philosophy, poetry, music, painting, sculpture, and romance, land of "starry climes and sunny skies," whose delicious climate, lofty mountains, and beautiful valleys and plains have ever excited the admiration of the traveller and poet, has made great progress in unity and freedom.

Suffrage nearly universal, the habeas corpus, freedom of religion and free schools are some of the principal features of Italian liberty.

The spirit of liberty is abroad in Russia—mighty empire of the North, whose government has represented the perfect idea of absolute despotism—an autocrat power, unrestrained by constitution or law. An enlightened Czar, animated by love for his people,

4

and perceiving the individual happiness and material prosperity produced by free institutions, abolished slavery throughout his dominions, made the serfs freemen, and gave to them local free institutions, based upon the right of suffrage. It is true the imperial power still extends over all—a dark, impenetrable canopy—but beneath its shadow there is individual liberty and local self-government. Thus far the prosperous result has established the wisdom of the Czar, and may we not believe that he has laid the foundation of a free government, to be developed into a grand republic in the far future?—and nearer, into a constitutional monarchy, with representative institutions? Liberty is like living seed; wherever planted it vivifies, expands, develops. Thus planted in Russia among the lowest people, and for local purposes, it will grow, develop, and finally conquer. Russia is among the progressive nations, and is our friend, and it was the American example which touched the heart and intellect of the Emperor.

The spirit of liberty in its onward march has invaded Spain, and is stirring the great national heart. We have lately seen the great Spanish people firmly, and almost peacefully and unanimously, depose a licentious Queen, and declare against her dynasty. We have seen this people meet in primary assemblies, and, by suffrage universal, elect a **National**

Cortes which has for many months, in calm debate, considered and framed a new constitution, which, although not republican in its form, contains so much liberty, so much that is good and progressive in government, as to give the world high hope in the future of Spain. We have heard this national assembly declare that all sovereignty and power reside in the people, thus denying the divine rights of kings, and asserting the fundamental idea of free institutions. We have heard it pronounce the abolition of slavery. We have heard it pronounce the right of all men to worship God according to the dictates of their own consciences. Verily, these are great things, and new times, in old Spain.

These are the germs of free institutions, and will, in the progress of years, grow into a republican government.

Cuba, the queen of the Antilles, richest gem in the Spanish crown, the most fertile of islands, rich beyond description in the fruits and productions of tropical climes, and from which the Spanish treasury has so long been supplied, is making a bold, vigorous, and. as we trust, a successful effort to throw off the Spanish yoke and establish her independence.

The native Cubans, inspired by the spirit of liberty, have proclaimed liberty to the slaves, freedom of religious opinion, and that governments exist only by the consent of the governed. Cuba belongs to the American system, and the question of her fate is essentially American. We cannot be indifferent to the struggle, and trust and believe that our Government stands ready to acknowledge her independence at the earliest moment that will be justified by the laws and usages of nations.

Though we cannot rightfully intervene between Spain and her colony which she has so long oppressed and impoverished, our sympathies are with the Cubans, and we cannot regret any aid they may receive which does not involve a breach of the international duty of our Government.

While the grand revolution in Spain is proceeding so peacefully and successfully; while the Spanish people are asserting their liberties and fortifying them by constitutional bulwarks, it is to be deeply regretted that they are denying to Cuba what they claim for themselves.

The American Revolution was also an English revolution. The struggle for liberty here reacted upon England, has gone forward there continually, and is stronger to-day than ever. One reform has succeeded another. The basis of suffrage has been widened from time to time, and has always been followed by an extension of the rights, privileges, and prosperity of the people. The institutions of England have become more liberal, just, and benefi-

cent as the right of suffrage has been extended, and
a larger number of men admitted to a voice in the
government. Recently we have seen a new extension of the franchise, followed almost immediately
by a movement for the disestablishment of the Irish
Church. The Irish Church establishment, though
professedly in the interests of Protestantism, is not
sustained or justified by the Protestant world, and
the Protestant masses of England are demanding
its repeal. The disestablishment bill has passed the
House of Commons, but the lords threaten to reject
it, or destroy it by modifications. It may sacrifice
itself, but it cannot thereby preserve the Irish establishment. The House of Lords is tolerated only
upon the condition that it will ratify the action of
the Commons, and will give its formal assent to all
popular movements. It possesses no real political
power, and will not be permitted to obstruct the
wishes of the people. Should it be rash enough to
reject the disestablishment bill, it will at once inaug-
urate a movement for its own reorganization, and
the destruction of hereditary privileges.

Such a movement cannot, perhaps, be long de-
ferred anyhow. Another reform bill will soon be
demanded, making suffrage universal, or nearly so,
to be followed by the disestablishment of the English Church, the abolition of the laws of primo-
geniture, and the final destruction of the kingly

office. The mass of the English people are substantially, though not professedly, republican in sentiment. They accept the great doctrine of human rights upon which our Government is founded; and, while they yet retain the throne and the House of Lords, any attempt on the part of either to exercise positive power, or resist the popular will, would be instantly met by threats of resistance, and, if not abandoned, by revolution. The throne and the Upper House remain much like the feudal castles that yet distinguish the English landscape, emblems of departed power, curious to the view, full of historic interest, but no longer dangerous to the peace of the surrounding country. English reforms, heretofore slow, are becoming more rapid, and the English people are marching with accelerated speed to a republican government. Universal suffrage and hereditary privilege cannot exist long together. They are essentially hostile elements. The progress of suffrage in England has been resisted at every step by the aristocratic classes; but after many years of struggle it has arrived at that point where its further progress cannot be long delayed. Universal suffrage lies at the very summit of the hill of Difficulty, the ascent of which is rugged, slow, and toilsome, but when achieved, the people will be masters of the situation. America is avenging herself upon England by gradually but surely overturning her aristocratic and hierarchic institutions by the force of her teachings and example. The principles of civil and religious liberty, crude and imperfect when first brought from England to America, having been refined, illustrated, and extended, we return them to the mother country for her adoption, ladened with rich and glorious results. The spirit of American liberty is abroad in England. Her Brights, Gladstones, Forsters, and her whole host of liberal statesmen are proclaiming the doctrines of the Declaration of Independence, and verifying the saying of a celebrated Englishman, that the American Revolution guaranteed the free institutions of England. We may not live to see England a republic, but I believe our children will. The event can be predicted with as much certainty as any other in human affairs, and it is hastening on, perhaps fast enough when all things are considered.

The difficulties in the way of putting down the rebel lion were great. The rebellious States contained a population of not less than ten millions, and although nearly four millions were slaves, yet most of them, until the very conclusion of the war, constituted the laboring and producing classes, and furnished the supplies for the rebel armies in the field, and the non-combatants at home. The territory of the rebellious States comprised an area of not less than eight hundred thousand square miles, diversified by vast ranges of mountains, deep rivers, tangled wilderness, and far-stretching swamps, and everywhere presenting natural defences, behind which a small force could hold a large one at bay.

The lines of communication were necessarily of great length, and maintained with difficulty. A large portion of our forces were constantly employed in this way, and in garrisoning posts, so that it was seldom we were able to meet the enemy with superior force upon the field.

These immense difficulties went far to counterbalance our superiority in population and resources, and were so great as to lead military observers throughout Europe to prophesy, almost with one accord, that we could not conquer the South. It was said there was no instance in history where so large a population, scattered over even one-third of a territory so great as that embraced by the rebellion, had been subdued. It was said we could not conquer space; that conquest would be a geographical impossibility; that three millions of men could not garrison the South, and that when we had captured their towns and overrun the inhabited parts of their country, they would still maintain the war in morass, mountain, and forest almost impenetrable to regular armies, until the North, exhausted in blood and treasure, and broken in hope, would give up the contest.

Such was the belief of leading military minds in Europe, and of the politicians of the South when the war began. These opinions seemed well-founded in reason and in history, and the suppression of the rebellion, all things considered, may be justly regarded as the greatest of all military achievements.

The fact that the rebels fought upon their own soil, in a country with which they were familiar, protected from the approach of loyal armies by the natural advantages before described, was a full compensation for the difference between the population and resources of the two sections, and the final triumph of our arms, and the suppression of the rebellion must be sought for in other causes.

What these causes were may be briefly stated:

First, In the strength, courage, and endurance imparted to armies by the conviction that they are fighting in a just and patriotic cause. The humblest privates in our army believed that they were fighting to preserve the best government in the world; to preserve liberty and extinguish slavery; in behalf of Civilization and Christianity; against Barbarism and Inhumanity. These convictions gave inspiration, courage, and hope to the army, and animated the great mass of the people of the North, who sustained the Government throughout the contest, constituting an immense moral power, in opposition to which the South had but little to offer.

The people of the South had bitter prejudices, which had been carefully fostered by the designing politicians. Many of them believed in the abstract doctrine, under the Constitution, of State sovereignty and the right of secession. Some of them believed in the rightfulness of slavery, but more in its profitableness, its convenience, and its contributions to luxury and pride. But all of these constituted no moral power to inspire the patriot, nerve the soldier, give consolation in the dying hour, or determine people never to surrender, and to struggle on to the last. When, therefore, the principal armies of the rebellion were overcome and had surrendered, the war was at an end. Hostility was not maintained in the forest and mountain, as had been predicted. The convictions, hopes, and purposes of the masses had been extinguished before their armies were, and although they were full of bitterness and humiliation, yet there was nothing left for which they might sacrifice their homes and the future quiet and prosperity of their lives. Their cause failed in advance of their armies and resources.

The rebel historian of the "Lost Cause," in descanting upon the subject, speaks as follows:

"The whole fabric of Confederate defence tumbled down at a stroke of arms that did not amount to a battle. There was no last great convulsion, such as usually marks the final struggle of a people's devotion, or the expiring hours of their desperation. The word surrender travelled from Virginia to Texas. A four years' contest terminated with the smallest incident of bloodshed; it lapsed, it passed by a rapid and easy transition, into a profound and abject submission. There must be some explanation of this flat conclusion of the war. It is easily found. Such a condition could only take place in the thorough demoralization of the armies and people of the Confederacy; there must have been a general decay of public spirit—a general rottenness of public affairs—when a great war was thus terminated, and a contest was abandoned so short of positive defeat, and so far from the historical necessity of subjugation."

And again he says:

"We fear that the lessons and examples of history are to the contrary, and we search in vain for one instance where a country of such extent as the Confederacy has been so thoroughly subdued by any amount of military force, unless where popular demoralization has supervened."

History records that many nations, far more exhausted than they, have struggled on to final victory. Our Revolutionary fathers, at the end of four years, defeated, exhausted and overrun, did not despair, but animated by the justice of their cause, and the belief that it would triumph because it was just, struggled on, and at the end of seven years were blessed with peace and the rich reward which shall be the inheritance of the earth. "Thrice is he armed who hath his quarrel just," and weak and defenceless are they who contend for injustice and slavery, though girt about by the mountain, the swift river, and the deep wilderness.

Secondly, The armies of the North were strong in that physical endurance which is communicated by habitual labor, and by that self-reliance and confidence which free labor only can inspire. They were strong in the intelligence of the masses who filled the ranks. These men understood well the nature of the struggle in which they were engaged. They knew the vast consequences to themselves, their posterity, and to the world, depending upon the result. Their education enabled them not only to comprehend the "cause," but military operations, the condition of the Government and the country, and the decline of the spirit and strength of the enemy. In short, our armies were a vast intelligence, subject to military control, possessing clear ideas of duty, condition, consequences, and spirit and resolution commensurate to these.

We have met here to-day to dedicate this Monument to the memory of the patriotic and gallant men who fell upon this field, and to testify our love to the great cause in which they perished. Their achievements will be recorded upon the pages of history, much more enduring than stone, but we desire to present this visible evidence of our remembrance and gratitude. We are surrounded to-day by many of the surviving heroes of the battle; by many of the relatives and friends of those beloved dead, and by many thousands of our people who rejoice in the preservation, peace and prosperity of our country. That we have a united country, that we have national Government, that we have peace in all our borders, that there is liberty and protection for all, that we have bright and glorious prospects of individual happiness and national growth and power, we owe to the brave men who fell upon this and other fields. The glorious circumstance and bright auspices over and around us to-day were purchased by their blood. We are in the full enjoyment of the prize for which it was shed. Let us increase the gratitude of our hearts by considering for a moment what would be our condition if the rebellion had triumphed. We would have no solemn but sweet occasions like this. We would have no common country, no common name, no national flag, no glorious prospects for the future.

Had the bond of union been broken the various

parts would have crumbled to pieces. We should have a slaveholding confederacy in the South; a republic on the Pacific; another in the Northwest, and another in the East. With the example of one successful secession, dismemberment of the balance would have speedily followed, and our country, once the hope of the world, the pride of our hearts, broken into hostile fragments, would have been blotted from the map, and became a byword among the nations. Let us thank Almighty God to-day, that we have escaped this horrible fate. We feel as one who awakes from a terrible dream, and rejoices that he is alive. We feel as did the children of Israel, when, standing upon the shores of the Red Sea, they looked back upon the destruction from which they had been delivered.

Mr. Lincoln, standing in this place a few months after the battle, and while yet the conflict was raging, dedicated himself to his country and to the cause of liberty and union. The demon of rebellion afterwards exacted his life, but the inspiration of the words he spoke is resting upon us to-day. The great prophecy he uttered when he said, "the nation shall, under God, have a new birth of freedom," and that "the government of the people, by the people, and for the people, shall not perish from the earth," is being fulfilled. He sealed his devotion with his blood, and sacred be his memory. The eloquent Everett, who spoke here on the same occasion, and who has since passed from earth, said: "God bless the Union; it is dearer to us from the blood of brave men which has been shed in its defence." As I stood by them and listened to their inspired words, my faith was renewed in the triumph of liberty; but imagination failed to stretch forward to this auspicious day. The march of events has been faster than our thoughts, and the fruits of victory have already exceeded our most sanguine expectations.

While we pay this tribute of love and gratitude to the dead, let us not forget the surviving heroes of the battle. They, too, offered their lives, but the sacrifice was not required. The admiration, love, and gratitude of the nation will attend them as they pass down the declivity of time to honored graves. In the evening of their lives they will tell the story of Gettysburg to wondering youth, who will listen as we did when our grandfathers told of Bunker Hill, Saratoga, and Yorktown. Many of them are here to-day, to review the scene of their struggle and triumph. How powerful the contrast between now and then! The dark cloud which overspread the horizon of the nation is gone, and all is brightness. The sulphurous cloud of battle, too, is gone, and there is nothing to obscure our vision of the field. The dead have returned to dust. The fields once cumbered with bodies and slippery with blood, are clothed with verdure and harvest, and to-day all is peace, beauty and repose.

We seek not to commemorate a triumph over our misguided countrymen. It is the cause we celebrate. Our triumph is theirs, and their children's children, until the latest generation. The great disturbing element has been removed. Vicious political heresies have been extirpated. The trial by wager of battle has been decided in favor of liberty and union, and all will submit. The people of the North and South have met each other face to face on many a field, have tried each others courage, have found they are much alike in many things, have increased their mutual respect, and are now preparing to live together more fraternally than before.

The Southern States are rapidly recovering from the prostration of the war, and with their deliverance from the incubus of slavery, with free labor, with free schools, with emigration from the North and from Europe, will soon attain a prosperity and power of which they scarcely dreamed in former days. The advancing prosperity is solid, just, and enduring. We rejoice in it. The bonds of union are made indissoluble by the community of political principles, by the complete identity of domestic and commercial interests, and by a uniform system of labor, of education, and of habits of thought and action. HENCEFORTH DISUNION IS IMPOSSIBLE.

DEDICATION ODE,

FOR THE NATIONAL CEMETERY AT GETTYSBURG,

July 1, 1869.

I.

After the eyes that looked, the lips that spake
Here, from the shadows of impending death,
Those words of solemn breath,
What voice may fitly break
The silence, doubly hallowed, left by him ?
We can but bow the head, with eyes grown dim,
And, as a nation's litany, repeat
The phrase his martyrdom hath made complete,
Noble as then, but now more sadly sweet ;
"Let us, the Living, rather dedicate
Ourselves to the unfinished work, which they
Thus far advanced so nobly on its way,
And save the periled State !
Let us, upon this field where they, the brave,
Their last full measure of devotion gave,   .
Highly resolve they have not died in vain !—
That under God, the nation's later birth
Of Freedom, and the People's gain
Of their own Sovereignty, shall never wane
And perish from the circle of the earth !"
From such a perfect text shall Song aspire
To light its faded fire,
And into wandering music turn

6

Its virtue, simple, sorrowful and stern ?
His voice all elegies anticipated :
For, whatsoe'er the strain,
We hear that one refrain :
"We consecrate ourselves to them, the Consecrated !"

II.

After the thunder-storm our heaven is blue :
Far-off, along the borders of the sky,
In silver folds the clouds of battle lie,
With soft, consoling sunlight shining through ;
And round the sweeping circles of your hills
The crashing cannon thrills
Have faded from the memory of the air ;
And Summer pours from unexhausted fountains
Her bliss on yonder mountains :
The camps are tenantless, the breastworks bare :
Earth keeps no stain where hero-blood was poured :
The hornets, humming on their wings of lead,
Have ceased to sting, their angry swarms are dead,
And, harmless in its scabbard, rusts the sword !

III.

Oh, not till now—oh, now we dare, at last,
To give our heroes fitting consecration !
Not till the soreness of the strife is past,
And Peace hath comforted the weary Nation !
So long her sad, indignant spirit held
One keen regret, one throb of pain unquelled,
So long the land about her feet was waste,
The ashes of the burning lay upon her,
We stood beside their graves with brows abased,
Waiting the purer mood to do them honor !
They, through the flames of this dread holocaust,
The patriot's wrath, the soldier's ardor, lost :
They sit above us and above our passion,
Disparaged even by our human tears,—
Beholding truth our race, perchance, may fashion

In the slow judgment of the creeping years.
We saw the still reproof upon their faces ;
We heard them whisper from the shining spaces :
"To-day ye grieve : come not to us with sorrow !
Wait for the glad, the reconciled To-morrow !
Your grief but clouds the ether where we dwell ;
Your anger keeps your souls and ours apart :
But come with peace and pardon, all is well !
And come with love, we touch you, heart to heart !"

IV.

Immortal Brothers, we have heard !
Our lips declare the reconciling word :
For Battle taught, that set us face to face,
The stubborn temper of the race,
And both, from fields no longer alien, come,
To grander action equally invited,—
Marshalled by Learning's trump, by Labor's drum,
In strife that purifies and makes united !
We force to build, the powers that would destroy :
The muscles, hardened by the sabre's grasp
Now give our hands a firmer clasp :
We bring not grief to you, but solemn joy !
And, feeling you so near,
Look forward with your eyes, divinely clear,
To some sublimely-perfect, sacred year,
When sons of fathers whom ye overcame
Forget in mutual pride the partial blame,
And join with us, to set the final crown
Upon your dear renown,—
The People's Union in heart and name !

V.

And yet, ye Dead !—and yet
Our clouded natures cling to one regret :
We are not all resigned
To yield, with even mind,
Our scarcely risen stars, that here untimely set.
We needs must think of history that waits
For lines that live but in their proud beginning—

Arrested promises and cheated fates—
Youth's boundless venture and its single winning.
We see the ghosts of deeds they might have done,
The phantom homes that beaconed their endeavor ;
The seeds of countless lives in them begun,
That might have multiplied for us forever !
We grudge the better strain of men
That proved itself, and was extinguished then—
The field, with strength and hope so thickly sown,
Wherefrom no other harvest shall be mown ;
For all the land, within its clasping seas,
Is poorer now in bravery and beauty,
Such wealth of manly loves and energies
Was given to teach us all the free man's sacred duty?

VI.

Again 'tis they, the Dead,
By whom our hearts are comforted.
Deep as the land-blown murmurs of the waves
The answer cometh from a thousand graves ;
"Not so ! we are not orphaned of our fate !
Though life was warmest and though love were sweetest,
We still have portion in their best estate ;
Our fortune is the fairest and completest !
Our homes are everywhere ; our loves are set
In hearts of man and woman, sweet and vernal :
Courage and Truth, the children we beget,
Unmixed of baser earth, shall be eternal.
A finer spirit in the blood shall give
The token of the lines wherein we live,—
Unselfish force, unconscious nobleness
That in the shocks of fortune stands unshaken,—
The hopes that in their very being bless,
The aspirations that to deeds awaken !
O, if superior virtue ye allow
To us, be sure it still is vital in you,—
That trust like ours shall ever lift the brow,
And strength like ours shall ever steel the sinew !

We are blossoms which the storm has cast
From the Spring promise of our Freedom's tree,
Pruning its overgrowths, that so, at last,
Its later fruit more bountiful shall be !—
Content, if, when the balm of Time assuages
The branch's hurt, some fragrance of our lives
In all the land survives,
And makes their memory sweet through still expanding ages !''

VII.

Thus grandly, they we mourn, themselves console us ;
And, as their spirits conquer and control us,
We hear, from some high realm that lies beyond,
The hero-voices of the Past respond.
From every State that reached a broader right
Through fiery gates of battle ; from the shock
Of old invasions on the People's rock ;
From tribes that stood, in Kings' and Priests' despite ;
From graves forgotten in the Syrian sand,
Or nameless barrows of the Northren strand,
Or gorges of the Alps and Pyrenees,
Or the dark bowels of devouring seas,—
Wherever Man for Man's sake died—wherever
Death stayed the march of upward-climbing feet,
Leaving their Present incomplete,
But through far Futures crowning their endeavor—
Their ghostly voices to our ears are sent,
As when the high note of the trumpet wrings
Æolian answers from the strings
Of many a mute, unfingered instrument.
Platæan cymbals thrill for us to-day ;
The horns of Sempach in our echoes play,
And nearer yet, and sharper, and more stern,
The slogan rings that startled Bannockburn ;
Till from the field, made green with kindred deed,
The shields are slashed in exultation
Above the dauntless Nation,
That for a Continent has fought its Runnymede !

VIII.

Yes, for a Continent! The heart that beats
With such rich blood of sacrifice
Shall, from the Tropics, drowsed with languid heats,
To the blue ramparts of the Northern ice,
Make felt its pulses, all this young world over !—
Shall thrill, and shake, and sway
Each land that bourgeons in the Western day,
Whatever flag may float, whatever shield may cover !
With fuller manhood every wind is rife,
In every soil are sown the seeds of valor,
Since out of death came forth such boundless life,
Such ruddy beauty out of anguished pallor !
And that war wasted arm
Put forth to lift a sister-land from harm,
Ere the last blood upon the blade was dried,
Shall still be stretched, to shelter and to guide,
Beyond her borders, answering the need
With counsel and with deed,
Along the Eastern and the Western wave,
Still strong to smite, still beautiful to save !

IX.

Thus, in her seat secure,
Where now no distant menaces can reach her,
At last in undivided freedom pure,
She sits, the unwilling world's unconscious teacher ;
And, day by day, beneath serener skies,
The unshaken pillars of her palace rise—
The Doric shafts, that lightly upward press,
And hide in grace their giant massiveness.
What though the sword has hewn each corner-stone,
And precious blood cements the deep foundation ?
Never by other force have empires grown ;
From other basis never rose a nation !
For strength is born of struggle, faith of doubt,
Of discord law, and freedom of oppression.
We hail from Pisgah. with exulting shout,

The Promised Land below us, bright with sun,
And deem its pastures won,
Ere toil and blood have earned us their possession !
Each aspiration of our human earth
Becomes an act through keenest pangs of birth ;
Each force, to bless, must cease to be a dream,
And conquer life through agony supreme :
Each inborn right must outwardly be tested
By stern material weapons, ere it stand
In the enduring fabric of the land,
Secured for those who yielded it, and those who wrested !

x.

This they have done for us who slumber here,
Awake, alive, though now so dumbly sleeping ;
Spreading the board, but tasting not its cheer,
Sowing, but never reaping ;—
Building, but never sitting in the shade
Of the strong mansion they have made ;—
Speaking their words of life with mighty tongue,
But hearing not the echo, million-voiced,
Of brothers who rejoiced,
From all our river-vales and mountains flung !
So take them, Heroes of the songful Past !
Open your ranks, let every shining troop
Its phantom banners droop,
To hail Earth's noblest martyrs, and her last !
Take them, O Fatherland !
Who, dying, conquered in thy name ;
And, with a grateful hand,
Inscribe their deed who took away thy blame,—
Give, for their grandest all, thine insufficient fame !
Take them, O God ! our Brave,
The glad fulfillers of Thy dread decree ;
Who grasped the sword for Peace, and smote to save,
And, dying here for Freedom, died for·Thee !

BAYARD TAYLOR.

BENEDICTION

REV. S. S. SCHMUCKER, D. D.

Exalted and adorable God. Once more we would lift up our souls in adoration to Thee, thou God of nations, who doest Thy will amongst the armies of heaven, and to whom the heaven, and the earth, and the whole universe of worlds owe their existence. Thy Almighty truth, O God, is irresistible, and Thy all-seeing eye is beholding the exercises of this solemn occasion. We have assembled here to-day to join in the exercises commemorative of the day, when, with outstretched arm Thou didst deliver Thy people, and the patriotism of those who have laid down their lives for the life of the nation, and whose bodies now sleep in these graves. There may they sleep in peace till the last trumpet shall sound and call the dead to judgment. We have come to pray for our country, and to pray to heaven for our misguided foes. O God, we pray Thee to banish from our land all elements of discord; may we be united by the cord of common brotherhood, and may our land continue to be an asylum for the oppressed and persecuted of all nations, until the day when Jesus Christ shall reign from the rising to the setting of the sun; and to Thy great name we will ascribe everlasting praise. *Amen.*

www.ingramcontent.com/pod-product-compliance
Lightning Source LLC
Chambersburg PA
CBHW030709110426
42739CB00031B/1365